Why?

Why is theory informed practice important?	28
Mapping practice	30
Promoting confidence	31
Why do people find theory informed practice problematic?	32
The way theory is taught	33
Language in social work theory	34
Fear and anxiety	36
Managerialist approaches to social work	38
Desire for certainty	40
Why should practitioners theorise?	42
Co-production of the social work knowledge base	44
Professionalising social work	48
'Bogged down' by theory?	51

How?

Theory and Practice: The Relationship	54
Theory Informed Practice: Wider Relationships	58
Evidence Based Practice	60
Reflective Practice	64
Knowledge and Social Work	68
Anti-oppressive Practice	71
Surface and Deep Approaches	72
Techniques and Exercises for developing theory informed practice	76
Using Supervision	106
Tips from Students	108
Meeting the challenges of theory informed writing	110
Eclecticism	114
Seeing the journey as continual	118
Putting it all together	120

The Social Work Pocket Guide to… Theory Informed Practice

By Siobhan Maclean

First Edition 2011 ISBN: 978-1-903575-76-5

A catalogue record for this book will be available from the British Library

©Kirwin Maclean Associates Ltd 4 Mesnes Green, Lichfield, Staffs, WS14 9AB

All Rights Reserved

No Reproduction, copy or transmission of this publication may be made without written permission.

No paragraph of this publication may be reproduced, or transmitted save with written permission or in accordance with the provision of the Copyright, Designs and Patents Act 1998.

Any person who does any unauthorised act in relation to this publication may be liable to criminal prosecution and civil claims for damages.

Printed in Great Britain by 4edge Limited.

Contents List...

What?

What is theory?	8
What is theoretical?	10
What is theorising?	11
My Eureka moment!	12
What does a theory do?	16
Formal and Informal theory	19
Theory and models	20
Theories *of* and theories *for* social work	23

WHAT?

In order to be able to implement effective theory informed practice, it is vital to understand what theory is. This pocket guide therefore begins by exploring the following questions:

- What is a theory?
- What is theorising?
- What is a method?
- What are the origins of theory?
- What does a theory do?

Thinking through these questions should help you to be clear about the starting point for theory informed practice:

WHAT IS THEORY INFORMED PRACTICE ALL ABOUT?

Theory is..............

What?

A theory is a set of ideas that helps to explain why something happens or happened in a particular way and to predict likely outcomes in the future. Theories are based on evidence and reasoning. but have not yet been conclusively proved.
(Cottrel 2005: 149)

.......a more or less well argued explanation of reality. Collectively, then, theories are explanations of reality or human behaviour or particular social phenomena, depending on the theory's central focus - that lead to particular interpretations of that reality. In other words, theorists offer particular explanations of reality that influence the ways in which people interpret situations or events.
(Gray and Webb 2009:10)

…..a set of ideas or principles used to guide practice, which are sufficiently coherent that they could if necessary be made explicit in a form which was open to challenge.
(Beckett 2006: 33)

> A theory makes assumptions about a behaviour, problem, target population or environment that are:
> - logical
> - consistent with everyday observations
> - similar to those used in previous successful interventions
> and
> - supported by past research in the same or related fields.
>
> (Croyle 2005)

> Theories in social care are nothing more than an attempt to explain social relationships. Theories have been developed since it became clear that there were similar patterns or repeating cycles of behaviours both in an individual's life and in the lives of lots of people.
>
> (Maclean 2006: 5)

> Fundamentally, theory is an attempt to explain a phenomenon or set of phenomena by providing a structured set of concepts that help us to understand the subject matter concerned.
>
> (Thompson 2010: 4)

Theoretical is:

> Concerned with or involving the examination of the theory of a particular subject or area of study. Restricted to theory rather than application.
> (American Heritage 2002)

> Theoretical thinking is about studying theory to look at how ideas can be generated, models can be suggested and hypotheses can be developed.
> (Skidmore 1979)

> Dealing with theories - distinguished from applying the theory.
> (Collins English Dictionary 2009)

What?

Theorising is:

> the way in which theory informs practice and practice can test and inform theory.
> (Thompson 2010)

> Theorising is, in a sense, a form of intervention, to the extent that it does not rest content with describing..... but opens itself to alternatives, what might-bes, as - ifs.
> (Young 1996)

> a form of action....... it can be about putting theory into practice..... or an abstraction of theory from practice..... an attempt to bring theory to 'heel'.... making theory relevant.
> (Clark, Dyson and Millward 1998)

My Eureka Moment!

Regular readers of the Social Work Pocket Guides will know that in seeking to understand concepts and ideas, I like to research the origins of words - I find it helps me to get a basic understanding of the concept. Theory is no different and many years ago when I was a social work student, I looked into the origins of the word theory.

The word originates from the Greek word "theoria", to which there are essentially two meanings:

- Going on a journey to see or experience something

- Looking at or beholding something and speculating and learning after seeing it.

What?

I must admit, that although I always still consider the origins of words, I didn't find looking at the origins of theory particularly enlightening as a student when I really struggled to understand and get to grips with theory informed practice.

In fact, my 'Eureka moment' came years later when talking to my friend Alison, who is a teacher. In sharing this Eureka moment, I don't wish to patronise any readers. It is very possible that this is something so basic that you've already considered it. However, for me, what Alison shared with me really helped.

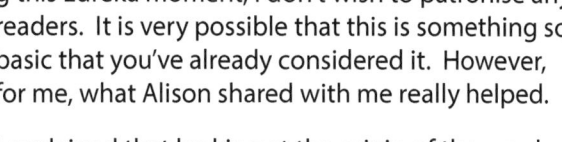

I explained that looking at the origin of the word hadn't helped me to understand the difference between theory, theoretical and theorising (as they all have the same origin). Alison said it's important not just to look at the origins of the word, but also to consider the "type" of word, and she took me through a basic grammar lesson:

- Theory is a noun.
- Theoretical is an adjective.
- Theorising is a verb.

and......

- a noun is a 'naming' word
- an adjective is a 'describing' word
- a verb is a 'doing' word

Eureka! After revisiting something I was taught at primary school (and obviously forgot!) I suddenly recognised the difference.

What?

Now why couldn't I have had that Eureka moment years ago when I was struggling to write assignments that made the links?

Theorising is when we put ideas into action and we develop ideas from action.

Being theoretical is about being able to describe and explore something.

A theory helps us to understand issues.

What does a theory do?

In science a theory is seen as being able to:

- **Describe:** What is happening?
- **Explain:** Why is it happening? How did this come about?
- **Predict:** What is likely to happen next?
- **Control and bring about change:** How can I intervene to change the likely outcome?

What?

In many ways this matches the social work role in assessment and planning:

Describe: In the assessment, we need to identify the presenting issues and understand the situation.

Explain: We need to analyse the information generated in the assessment in order to understand how the situation came about and why things are as they are.

Predict: We are often (particularly in risk assessment) asked to make predictions about what might happen in the future.

Control and bring about change: Whilst (because of the power connotations) I would change the word 'control' to 'intervene' - we generally develop plans to intervene in a situation and bring about some change.

Formal and Informal Theory

A number of writers in social work separate theory into formal and informal theory (see for example, Beckett 2006 and Thompson 2010).

Some people use these terms inappropriately – with formal theory being taken to mean theory which is presented more academically and is perhaps therefore difficult to access and informal theory being taken to mean theory which is more accessible and understandable. However, this is a misunderstanding.

Formal theory is basically any theory which can be traced back to a writer. Thompson (2010) argues that formal theory is explicit and open to question and critique), such that it has a level of "intellectual credibility" associated with it.

Informal theory on the other hand, is the worker's own ideas about a situation. As such this is often developed through experience – both practice

What?

experiences and personal experiences. This developed understanding is often referred to as practice wisdom (Doel and Shardlow 1993) or common knowledge (Beckett 2006). In my view informal theory often contains elements of formal theory which have seeped into the practitioner's practice and many social workers and students use a range of practice wisdom which actually contains both formal and informal theory.

Well rounded theory informed practice should involve drawing on both formal and informal theory. It should also be about making use of practice wisdom and further developing that practice wisdom.

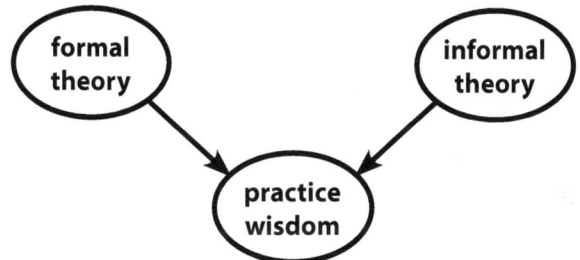

Theory and Models

There is often a confusion in social work about the difference between a theory and a model.

I find that the framework outlined on page 16 can help to clarify this. In my view, a 'theory' helps to answer the describe, explain and predict aspects of this framework and a model helps to answer the intervene and bring about change aspect.

Another way of looking at this is to use the What? Why? How? questions that form the basis of the social work pocket guide series. A theory helps a practitioner to answer the 'What?' and 'Why?', while a model helps to answer the 'How?'

> The essential difference between theories and models is that theories help us to understand a situation whilst models give an idea about what we can do.

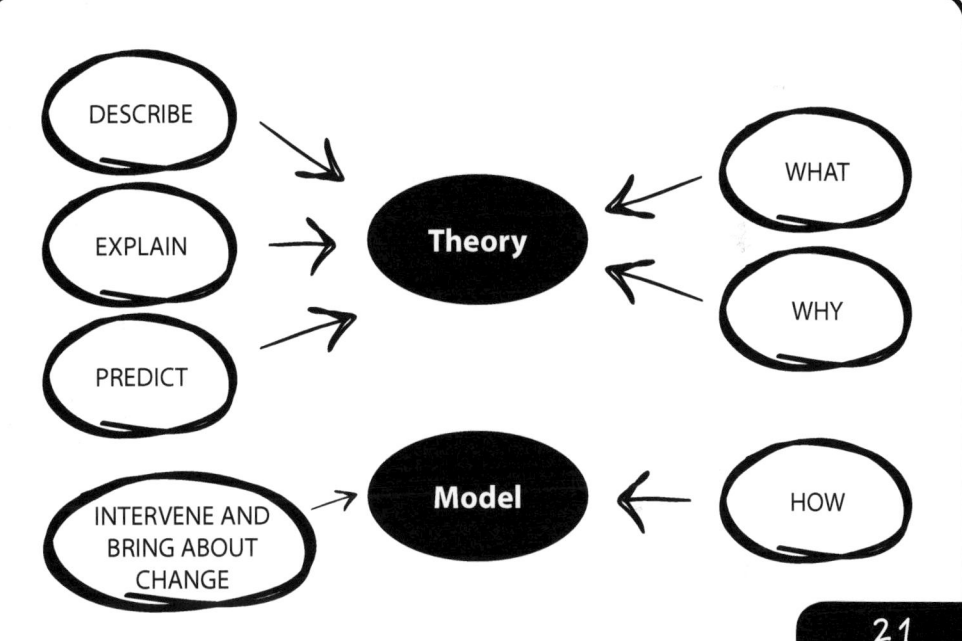

Walsh (2010) offers a useful figure to illustrate the relationship of theory to practice. It can also be helpful in understanding the differences between a theory and a model.

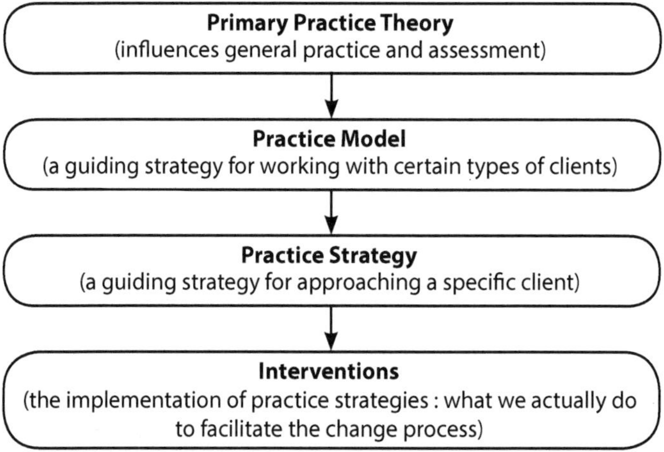

Primary Practice Theory
(influences general practice and assessment)

↓

Practice Model
(a guiding strategy for working with certain types of clients)

↓

Practice Strategy
(a guiding strategy for approaching a specific client)

↓

Interventions
(the implementation of practice strategies : what we actually do to facilitate the change process)

Theories *of* and theories *for* social work

One common idea about the different forms of social work theory is that there are theories *of* social work and theories *for* social work.

In straightforward terms, this means that there are theories about the way social work is delivered which constitute theories *of* social work (for example, task centred practice, group work, crisis intervention etc). Theories *for* social work are essentially theories which a social worker can use to explain situations, behaviours etc (such as attachment, systems behaviourism etc).

Collingwood (2011) describes theories *of* and *for* social work using the terms:

- **theory to inform** — equipping the practitioner with an understanding of the service user's situation — **theories *for* social work**

- **theory to intervene** — enabling the practitioner to intervene in the service user's situation — **theories *of* social work**

What?

Sibeon (1989) takes this idea further and proposes a three part distinction between theories in social work:

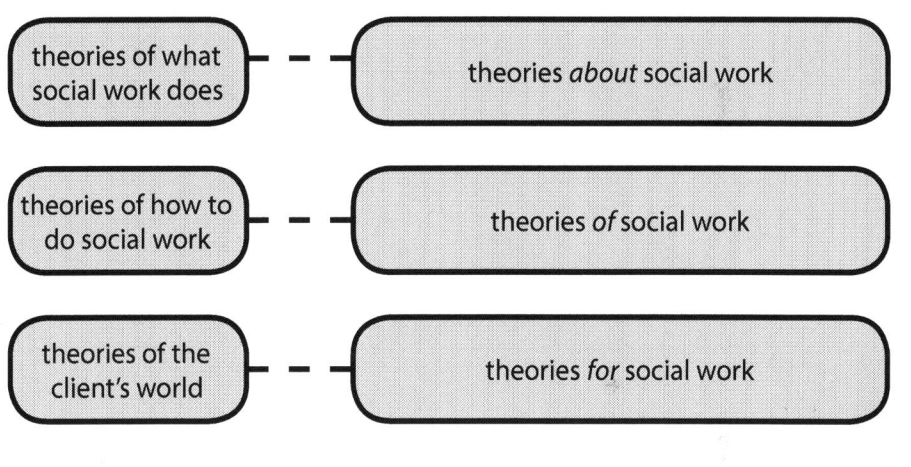

If you are going to use something to inform your practice, clearly you need to know what that 'something' is. Not only do you need to understand the specific and various theories you will draw on, but you also need to know what the concept of a theory in general terms is.

Understanding what a theory is and what you should be able to do with it is the first (vital) step on the journey towards theory informed practice.

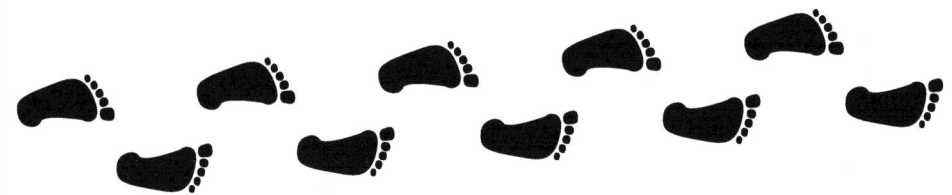

WHY?

Theory informed practice is rejected by a number of students and practitioners who see themselves as "practical" or as "hands on practitioners" who want to get on with "the job." In exploring the following questions:

- Why is theory informed practice important to social work?
- Why should practitioners theorise?
- Why do social workers find theory informed practice problematic?

This section should help you identify why theory is so important as part of effective social work practice.

WHY IS THEORY INFORMED PRACTICE SO IMPORTANT IN SOCIAL WORK?

Why is theory informed practice important?

Theory can help us to understand people, which in turn helps us to establish better working relationships with people.

Using theory can help to justify practice - and explain the reasons behind actions to service users, managers and society in general. The aim is that this will lead to social work becoming more effectively accountable.

Using a theory can give a reason about why an action resulted in a particular consequence. This can help us review and possibly change practice in an attempt to make the consequences more effective.

When working with individuals, making use of the theories which may relate to their specific situation can give more direction to our work.

Theory can help us to explore situations - we can generate ideas about what is happening and what we can do to bring about change.

Why?

- Changes in the profession, particularly in service delivery, may well be influenced by a theory. Therefore understanding theory can help us to anticipate likely future changes to the profession and our work.

- The development of a more cohesive knowledge base around theory will support the development of a more cohesive profession.

- Theory helps us to consider the context of our practice - for example the societal and cultural context in which we are working can become clearer.

- Theory informed practice can increase a practitioner's confidence and job satisfaction.

"Mapping" practice

There is an old saying started by Leonardo Da Vinci *"Practice without theory is to sail an uncharted sea. Theory without practice is not to set sail at all"*.

Imagine a boat setting out to sea in a good breeze, without a map or a compass. This is like practice without theory - how will the crew know when they have arrived at their destination? If, by some remote chance they arrive safely in a port they like, how would they ever be able to repeat the journey? On the other hand, a boat might bob along tied to its bollard, safe in the harbour. It might well have every direction finding device known, but it isn't going anywhere. This is like theory without practice. It's pointless.

Why?

Promoting Confidence

There is no doubt that theory informed practice has an impact on practitioners confidence. Thompson (2010) asserts that theory helps to build two types of confidence:

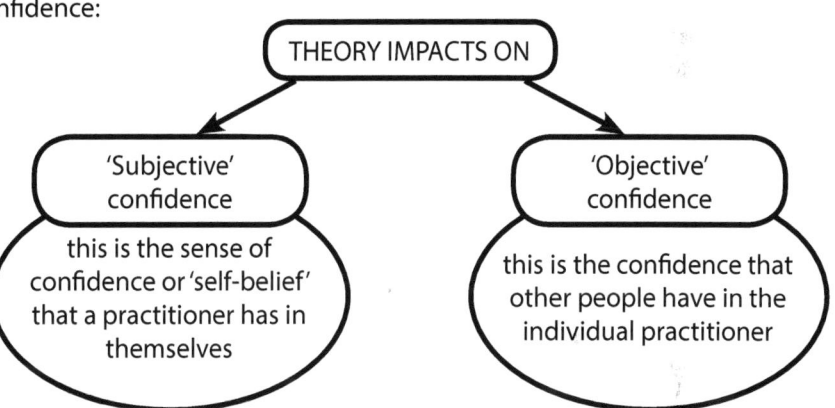

Why do people find theory informed practice problematic?

Watson, Burrows and Player (2002) describe integrating theory and practice as a constantly "knotty problem". Theory informed practice is certainly something which has challenged students and practitioners over the years - but why is it such a "knotty problem"?

- complexities of language
- fear and anxiety
- the way theory is taught
- managerialist approaches to social work
- desire for 'certainty'

Why?

The way theory is taught

Whilst the requirements for social work training state that all social work programmes must *"Ensure that the teaching of theoretical knowledge, skills and values is based on their application to practice."* (Department of Health 2002:3)

"IF THEORIES ARE RECIPES, STUDENTS OFTEN EAT BUT NEVER COOK."

Many social work students find that theory is taught in a way which they find difficult to apply to their practice.

Lopez (2011) explains that theory is typically taught in a way which presents theories "as recipes" whilst students are rarely taught to cook.

Language in social work theory

In 1926 the French writer Antoine de Saint-Exupery famously said "language is the source of most misunderstandings." Good social workers recognise the vital importance of language in clear communication and they are well aware of the way that language (particularly what we commonly refer to as jargon) can be used to exclude people.

This leaves me wondering why social work academics appear to seek out the most complex form of language when they are writing about theory. Thompson (2010) refers to the language used in theory as 'academic code' and he recognises that theory can be expressed using a language that "excludes people who are not members of a certain club".

As a practitioner, not an academic, I often feel as though I'm left "outside the club". As a student, this made me concerned about my abilities to understand key concepts in social work. As an experienced practitioner however, I have developed the confidence to recognise that it says more about the failure of the writers to communicate clearly.

When I have had the opportunity to talk to academics about why they write in this way, they generally refer to the need for improved intellectualism in social work and the danger of 'over simplifying' concepts.

However, I would argue that as practitioners, we do not 'over simplify' the issues we discuss with service users and yet we seek to meet the challenge of communicating clearly in a way which does not de-personalise and does not exclude.

I am reminded of the famous quotation by Albert Einstein who developed what is probably the most famous theory of all (the theory of relativity):

"A theory is the more impressive the greater is the simplicity of its premises, the more different are the kinds of things it relates to and the more extended the range of its applicability."

(Einstein, undated)

Fear and anxiety

Students and practitioners alike often appear almost "afraid" of theory and there is certainly anxiety about theory informed practice.

> I was frightened of the word theory.
> (Simms 2009)

> I can honestly say that when I started the course, attempting to read social work theory sent me into a state of panic!
> (McConnachie 2009)

> I found theory informed practice daunting and dreaded my practice educator asking me about theory.
> (Bibi 2009)

Why?

As the University of York (2000) point out, anxiety can impede learning. Apprehension on the other hand, can enhance learning. To be able to adopt a theory informed approach to practice then, it is vital that practitioners address any fears they have about theory.

- ✘ Don't avoid the subject of theory
- ✘ Read around and find an author who brings theory to life for you
- ✘ Talk about your concerns to others - you'll find many others share your concerns
- ✘ Reflect on your fears and anxieties - exactly what is it you are frightened of?
- ✘ Recognise the importance of theory informed practice
- ✘ Use some of the tips and ideas covered in the 'How?' section of this pocket guide to develop your confidence around theory

Managerialist approaches to social work

Much has been written about the rise of the managerialist approach in contemporary social work (see for example, Scottish Government 2011 and Kirkpatrick 2006). Characterised by case management, accountability, targets and evidence based practice, managerialism is seen as removing creativity and theorising from practice.

"Social work has become legalised and proceduralised and there have been increasing efforts to scientise and rationalise practice and emphasise empiricism, outcomes and the evidence based movement."

(Parton 2011)

Certainly, when I talk to social work practitioners about their work, they are very quickly able to identify the legislation and policy which informs their work. They are often much less enthusiastic about the theory that informs their practice and ready to identify and discuss this.

Why?

Supervision of qualified workers tends to focus on the managerialist agenda - audit, targets, policy and taking on more work! Once a practitioner completes their qualification, they are very rarely (if ever!) asked the question that students dread "and what theory are you using?"

In fact Jacqui Smith, former Minister of Social Care (quoted in Singh and Cowden 2009: 4) said:

"Social work is a very practical job. It is about protecting people and changing their lives, not about being able to give a fluent and theoretical explanation about why they got into difficulties in the first place."

My view would be that it is not possible to support people to "change their lives" without a "fluent" and clear understanding of the way that theory can support this - and the options that are possible.

Good social work is about much more than a 'conveyor belt' approach. Practice should be well supported within a framework of theory and evidence as well as policy and legislation.

Desire for certainty

Linked to the rise of managerialism, the focus in contemporary social work seems to be on finding the 'right' answer and a desire for certainty.

Theory does not offer certainty and certainly it cannot give the 'right' answer. In fact as Ife (2005) says there is no 'right answer' but there are potentially lots of right answers.

Effective theory informed practice is actually about a process of dynamic questioning. Reflective, theory informed practice creates questions about questions. It does not always provide answers to those questions. This does not sit particularly comfortably in a world where managers want confident action and don't want to know that practitioners have unanswered questions. Social workers often fear uncertainty and may avoid theory informed practice because the uncertainty created does not sit comfortably. However, "staying with the uncertainty" (Ixer 2010) is an important aspect of being a truly reflective practitioner.

This willingness to work with uncertainty is a key part of being a professional and

Why?

has long been recognised in established professions like medicine. Seedhouse (1998) stated that a *"willingness to work with uncertainty is at the heart of healthcare".*

In medicine, the inter-relationship between theory and practice is perhaps more clearly defined than it is in social work. For example, Jones (1999) explains that in medicine, theory is about trying to deduce why someone has become ill (the causes and nature of illness), whereas practice is about making someone healthy. The two are inter-related in that it is possible to theorise without 'curing' specific patients and it is possible to 'cure' a patient without knowing exactly how the cure worked. This clear inter-relationship is perhaps why the medical profession is more comfortable with uncertainty than social workers practising in a managerialist culture.

In citing this example, I am not suggesting that social work should take a medical model approach - nor that we should seek to 'cure' service users. Simply that, at times, when social work is under attack and moves towards professionalisation are unclear, it may be worth us looking towards how other professions view the relationship between theory and practice.

Why should practitioners theorise?

According to Thompson (2010) *"to do social work is to theorize practice (to draw on sets of ideas to make sense of it) and to practice theory (to make use of those ideas in a practical context)."*

I've yet to come across a social worker who describes the key aspect of their job as 'theorising'. However, I would agree with Thompson in that I see theorising as an essential aspect of social work practice. There are various reasons for this, including:

- Professionalising social work
- Checking the 'practice validity' of theory
- Co-production of the social work knowledge base

Why?

Practice Validity

In just the same way that theory should inform practice, it is vital that practice should inform theory. Sheppard (1998) refers to whether theory has a 'practice validity'. It is only service users and practitioners who will really know whether a theory works in practice (in other words whether it has a validity).

If we return to Lopez's analogy of theories as recipes and theorising as cooking - surely practitioners have the responsibility to let academics know if the food tastes terrible!

"WE HAVE A RESPONSIBILITY TO LET ACADEMICS KNOW IF THE FOOD TASTES TERRIBLE..."

Co-production of the social work knowledge base

Contemporary social work practice recognises the vital importance of working in close partnership with service users and doing things 'with' rather than 'to' service users. We seek to 'co-produce' assessments and intervention plans with service users. It concerns me that as a profession, we seem to be prepared to allow a continued paternalistic 'top down' approach to the production of the social work knowledge base.

Thompson (2010: 247) asserts that:

"If we are to safeguard our professionalism in the face of bureaucratizing tendencies, then we need to make sure that the knowledge base is as sound as it can be and as fully geared up to addressing the challenges of managerialism as it reasonably can be."

Social workers who do not theorise, risk leaving the profession open to a 'top down' approach to theory development. We have a vitally important role to play in the development of social work theory and as practitioners, we need to take up the challenge.

Why?

The British Association of Social Workers recognise that practitioners need to work in partnership with social work academics to co-produce the social work knowledge base and in 2011 instigated a project entitled "Empowering Social Work Practitioners: Sharing Practice Wisdom". This involves an annual social work practitioner symposium. In 2011 twenty seven practitioners presented their practice wisdom, demonstrating their commitment to theorising and contributing to the social work knowledge base. The contributors and participants of the Symposium identified that whilst there were challenges and barriers to theorising as practitioners, there were also a range of solutions, including:

- mentoring and support
- improving links between Universities and practice environments
- training opportunities
- supportive/enabling environments
- affirmation of professional status and expertise
- reflective practice

(BASW 2011)

The Theory Doughnut

As a visual thinker, I like the concept of the theory doughnut. Parton (1994: 30) stated that:

"increasingly it feels as if social work does not have a core theoretical knowledge base and that there is a hole in the centre of the enterprise."

Reflecting on this book so far, food seems to be a central analogy (I wonder if my diet is having an impact!) However, Parton's words do remind me of a doughnut. Maybe it's because jam doughnuts have always been my favourite and I've never been keen on the ones with the hole in the middle - but I do strongly believe we have a responsibility, as social work practitioners, to fill in that hole!

Why?

Much of the theory used in social work practice is drawn from different disciplines - predominantly sociology, psychology, health and education. This can mean that the values of social work are missing - perhaps this is the hole at the centre of the theory doughnut. Certainly, Singh and Cowden (2009: 8) argue that "simply 'defending values' can become somewhat hollow." Ensuring that values are integral to the use of theory in social work practice is an important role for the theory informed practitioner.

Theorising on practice can help fill in the hole and provide a more robust theoretical base for social work.

Professionalising Social Work

In recent years, there has been significant discussion about the 'professionalisation' of social work. Despite this, as Green (2006) explains, social work is still viewed as a 'pariah profession' with a poor intellectual standing. Alongside the debate about the need to raise the professional standing of social work, there has been a move towards more technical competency-based assessment. In England, the Social Work Taskforce recommended a professional capabilities framework for social work which goes from the point of entry to social work training, through the various career stages in social work to team manager level. This framework could be seen as adding further levels of 'technical competence'.

This move towards professionalism on the one hand and technicality on the other, has led to some confusion within the profession, with Singh and Cowden (2009: 13) arguing that *"while professionalism must be mobilised in the defence of the autonomy of decision-making, we also need to ask what kind of professionalism we need to be articulating."*

Why?

Singh and Cowden (2009) argue that contemporary definitions of social work, such as that articulated by Jacqui Smith (see page 39) assume that 'thinking' and 'doing' are separate activities. The first draft of the Health and Social Care Bill put before the Westminster Parliament earlier this year described social work as: *"Social work is what social workers do."*

Whilst this trite definition could be argued on many levels, it is important to recognise that as well as 'doing', social workers also 'think'. As a profession, we need to be free to think and making full use of theory - and developing theory from our practice is the only way to do this.

Singh and Cowden (2009) argue that social work is an intellectual profession which synthesises theoretical and practical, and argue for social workers to be seen as *"transformative intellectuals who do not succumb to power, but engage in uncovering, confronting and resisting power."*

> What we think informs what we do.

The Munro review of child protection (2011) recognised the need for social work to enhance its professional identity, recommending a move towards more preventative work (informed by theories and models for effective intervention). However, as Megele (2011) states:

"....... if social work is to truly enhance its professional identity, image and status, it must overcome the anti-intellectualism in its practice and reconcile the divide between theory and professional day-to-day practice...... Until we do, we have little hope of living up to Professor Munro's vision of social workers as trusted and independent professionals."

Whatever 'kind' of professionalism we are working towards, it is clear that being a professional involves synthesising 'thinking' and 'doing' (for example see Schön 1983).

Theory informed practice is therefore an essential aspect of developing a strong profession of social work to meet the challenges of the future.

Why?

'Bogged' Down by Theory?

To conclude this section of the Pocket Guide, it's worth looking at the concept of being 'bogged down' by theory. This is a term you often hear in relation to theory informed practice. In fact, it's regularly used in marketing tactics, to sell books to social work students - for example, I've read a number of reviews and sales pitches for social work books which say things like *"this is a practical book which is not bogged down by theory......."*

Using terms like this will only further the 'anti-intellectual' trends in social work and the rejection of theory by social workers. The imagery around being 'bogged down' by theory suggests that it is something to avoid (that we should walk around the 'boggy' area).

HOW?

There is no single approach to theory informed practice, so it is important for individual workers to find a method that works for them. This section therefore explores a range of methods which can be used to develop skills in theory informed practice. By considering the following questions:

- Do we apply, link or integrate theory with practice?
- What methods can social workers use to develop theory informed practice?
- What are the links between reflective practice, evidence based practice and theory informed practice?

This section should help you to look at what is perhaps the most important question of all:

HOW DO I DO IT?

Theory and Practice: The Relationship

The 'What?' section of this pocket guide began to consider the links between theory and practice in social work. However, before considering how social workers can develop their skills in theory informed practice, it is important to consider the relationship between the two.

Thompson (2010) argues simply and perhaps therefore powerfully, that theory and practice are "two sides of the same coin."

"THEORY AND PRACTICE ARE 2 SIDES OF THE SAME COIN."

How?

However, relationships are never simple, which social workers clearly recognise in their practice. Fook (2002) asserts that the relationship between theory and practice is much more complex and intermingled than a simple split construction of them suggest.

Maidment and Egan (2009) consider the relationship between theory and practice to be *"symbiotic, ever-changing and reflexive."*

Giroux (2003: 38) asserts that *"theory....... requires a certain distance from practice. Theory and practice represent a particular alliance, not a unity in which one is dissolved into the other."*

There are therefore many different views about the relationship between theory and practice, which can make theory informed practice more complex for social workers. The starting point for effective theory informed practice is for a practitioner to decide how they view the relationship between theory and practice.

"THEORY AND PRACTICE DO NOT SIMPLY DISSOLVE INTO EACH OTHER"

Various terms are used in terms of the relationship between theory and practice. For example, social work literature refers to:

- applying theory to practice
- linking theory with practice
- integrating theory and practice
- theorising social work practice
- synthesising theory and practice

With so many words and terms in use, it's no wonder that as practitioners we are sometimes left unsure about what to do with theory!

Using visual representations of this can help to understand how theory and practice are often viewed.

Applying theory to practice:

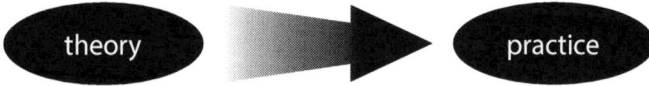

Linking theory with practice:

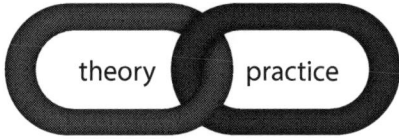

Theorising practice:

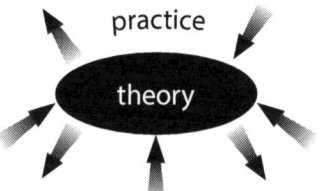

Theory Informed Practice: Wider Relationships

Theory is not the only thing which should inform a social worker's practice. Good practice should be informed by:

- theory
- law and policy
- research
- a wide ranging knowledge base
- critical reflection
- values and ethics

Therefore, not only is there a relationship between theory and practice, but there are also wider relationships with concepts such as reflective practice, evidence based practice and anti-oppressive practice.

How?

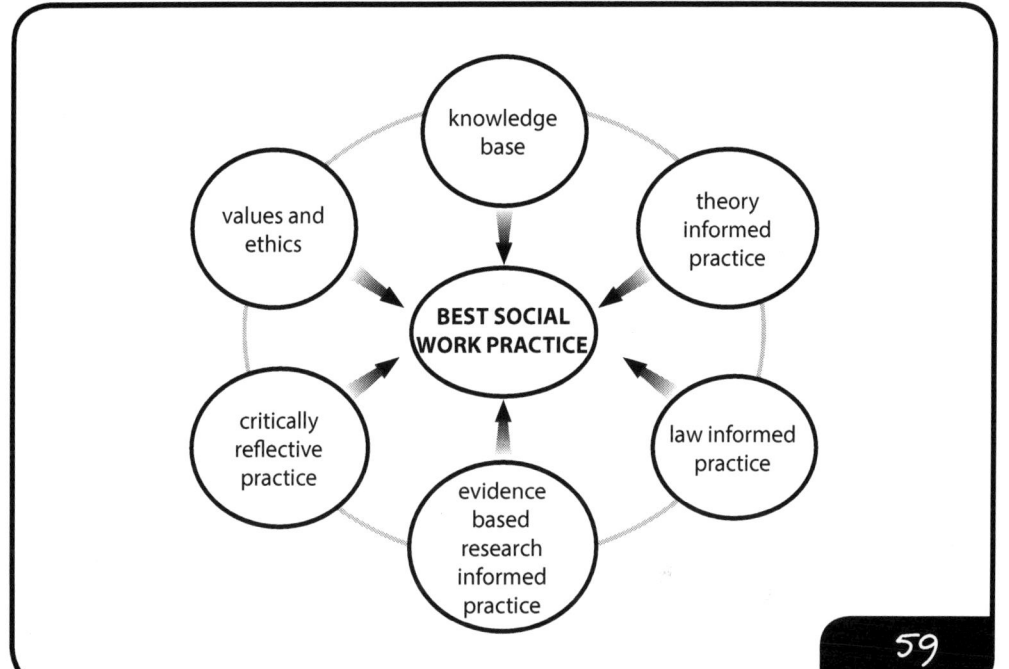

Evidence Based Practice

Originating in health care, evidence based practice has a growing prominence in social work. However, there are extensive debates in social work about what exactly evidence based practice is (Gray, Plath and Webb 2009). The Canadian medical group at McMaster University, who first coined the phrase, defined evidence based practice as a process which considers:

"the conscientious, explicit and judicious use of current best evidence in making decisions about the care of individuals."

(Sackett, Straus, Richardson, Rosenberg and Haynes 1997)

In practice, evidence based practice is often viewed by social workers as being about the use of research. However, I would use the term research informed practice for this. I see evidence based practice as wider than this.

A number of writers support the spread of evidence based practice in social work. For example, Forrester (2010) states that the solution to current difficulties in the way that social work is perceived should be addressed by three actions:

1. Developing an evidence base to tell us 'what works' in social work.
2. Commitment to using evidence based ways of working (which may mean workers being expected to use specific approaches).
3. Focus of professional evidence in developing and delivering evidence based approaches.

However, Webb (2001) argues that social workers engage in a complex *"reflexive understanding and not a determinate or certainty based decision-making process based on objective evidence"* and asserts that the current evidence-based "pre-occupation" in the profession "entraps" social workers into mechanistic ways of working which are unsatisfactory.

Returning to the analogy of food which seems to run throughout this Pocket Guide - Smith (2004) draws on Sheldon's metaphor of a recipe and points out that recipes in a cook book can be followed by anybody, so the dish prepared should be predictable and reliable. However, in practice, dishes turn out differently which might be about the cook's skills or expertise. Whilst the evidence (recipe) that workers use might be the same, the outcomes for service users will differ significantly.

There are clear and valid arguments, both for and against the use of evidence based practice in social work. In my view, there is an important place in social work for evidence based practice, but this should be viewed in addition to, rather than instead of, theory informed practice.

The English Government says of evidence based practice:

"Crucially, evidence-based practice involves the integration of the individual practitioner or clinician's expertise with the best available evidence from research, as well as with the preferences of the individual client or patient."
(Department for Children, Schools and Families 2008)

Whilst Gray, Plath and Webb (2009) make it clear that evidence based practice should be located within the traditions of social work theories, ethics and practice principles. The Journal of Evidence Based Social Work also recognises the value of theory in evidence based practice with the Taylor and Francis Group (2011) saying that the Journal views evidence based practice as evaluating cutting-edge theory, techniques and strategies.

How?

Evidence based practice and theory informed practice are often seen as opposed and in conflict. However, it is important for social workers to find common ground between the two. These are not opposing approaches but can be used in conjunction with each other.

In fact, the historical developments of theory informed practice and research informed practice have much in common. As Megele (2011) explains: *"research into social work is often carried out in areas such as sociology, social policy and psychology. This has hindered a greater appreciation and development of the specific foundations of social work."*

To develop a strong and resilient profession, we need to ensure that both theory and research evidence are developed from within the profession. It is important therefore that social workers begin to recognise the potential value of both approaches to avoid having evidence and theory (which may not fit) imposed upon the profession.

Reflective Practice

Whilst it is generally agreed that reflective practice is an essential aspect of good practice in social work, there is very little agreement on the concept and defining reflective practice is not a straightforward task (see Maclean 2010). There is however, a clarity about the relationship between theory and reflective practice.

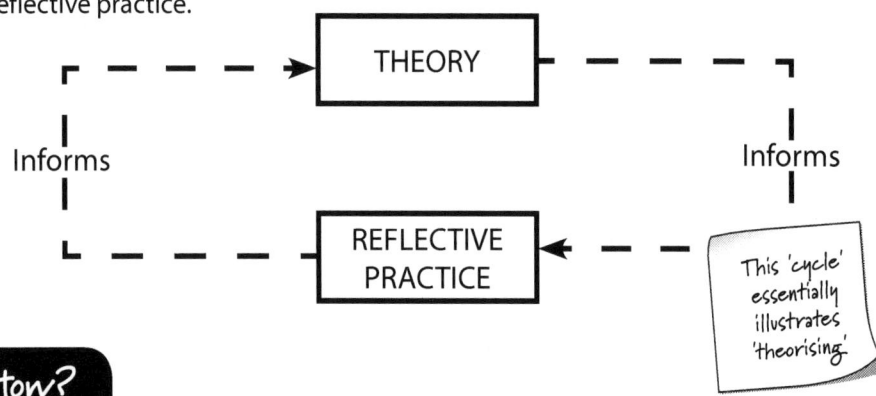

How?

Theory and Reflective Practice

Biggs (1999: 6) explains that "a reflection in a mirror is an exact replica of what is in front of it. Reflection in professional practice, however, gives back not what it *is*, but what it *might be*, an improvement on the original."

Reflective practice therefore opens up possibilities. It provides a range of options - rather than simply prescribing a single idea.

IN SOCIAL WORK REFLECTIVE PRACTICE THROWS UP MANY POSSIBILITIES

One area which 'opens up' possibilities for social work practice is theory. It is therefore essential for social workers to draw on their understanding of theory in the reflective process.

However, it is important that social workers take a critical approach to the use of theory in their practice, as Ife (2005) says:

"Whatever the theory or model, the social worker has a strong responsibility always to engage in critical and informed reflection on the context, the issues, the people involved, and on his / her practice."

and this is where reflective practice can begin to inform theory:

Critical reflection should inform theory in a number of ways. For example,

- Reflecting on theory can test its practice validity (see page 43)
- Reflecting on practice supports social workers to theorise. As Smith (2004) clearly identifies *"professional expertise therefore involves the ability to reflect upon and develop theory from practice."*

How?

For practitioners struggling to recognise the links between reflective practice and theory informed practice, a good example can be drawn from Jan Fook's work. She is perhaps the most well known contemporary writer on reflective practice in social work.

Fook (2002) emphasises the importance of the practitioner reflecting on power dynamics and exploring the impact of these in practice when 'deconstructing' a situation as part of the reflective process. Clearly, this means that theories of power must be considered in the reflective process. In 'reconstructing' the situation at the end of the process, Fook says the worker should be able to view the situation differently (particularly in terms of power). This is where the worker is beginning to develop their own theory from their practice.

Knowledge and social work

Effective social work practice should be informed by a wide range of knowledge - for example a practitioner needs to have a good working knowledge of the legal framework underpinning their practice.

Boddy and Statham draw on a range of research studies to identify the knowledge and education required for effective practice in social care. They note a distinction between three forms of knowledge:

Tacit knowledge: Sometimes referred to as practice wisdom, this is the knowledge derived from experience and personal qualities.

Functional knowledge: This is the knowledge which might be specifically required to perform defined tasks to an agreed standard. This is the kind of knowledge which has historically featured most heavily in competence based qualifications.

How?

Professional knowledge: This type of knowledge is described as combining professional skills (including specific competencies) and practical experience with a strong theoretical underpinning.

(Boddy and Statham 2009: 13)

Boddy and Statham's research review clearly identifies the importance of knowledge around theory to social work practice.

Knowledge can also be seen in terms of horizontal and vertical knowledge (Maclean and Caffrey 2009). This is a concept drawn from information technology, where the two forms of knowledge can be defined in different ways. In terms of social work, I would define vertical knowledge as that which is specific to a particular profession - for example, social work, nursing, education etc. As such, it is knowledge that all social workers will share - regardless of the service user group they work with (for example, knowledge about theories of power, oppression and understanding human behaviours). Horizontal knowledge, on the other hand, is specialised knowledge about a particular service user group.

This knowledge will not be specific to social workers, but will be shared by a range of different professionals working with a specific group. For example, specific knowledge about models of dementia and approaches to intervene will be shared by a variety of professionals working with people with dementia.

As social workers develop their knowledge of theory on both a horizontal and vertical basis the wide range of theoretical options will become clear.

Wide range of theories

HORIZONTAL KNOWLEDGE

VERTICAL KNOWLEDGE

How?

Anti-oppressive Practice

Clifford and Burke (2008) explain the importance of using an understanding of theory to work in an ethical anti-oppressive way and they consider how theories can be explored using an ethical framework. Thus, demonstrating the cyclical relationship between anti-oppressive practice and theory informed practice, in that:

 Theory informs anti-oppressive practice: It is important to understand theories of power, oppression, ethics and practice in order to work in an anti-oppressive way.

 Anti-oppressive practice should inform theory: Much of the theory used in social work practice is drawn from outside of the profession. Theory may have its roots in sociology, health, psychology or management. As such, it is unlikely to reflect the values of social work and it is the practitioner's responsibility to incorporate these into their use of the theory.

Surface and Deep Approaches

Marton and Saljo (1976) identified the concept of deep learning and surface learning.

Surface Approach: This focuses on acquiring and memorising information. An uncritical, unquestioning approach is taken to acquiring new knowledge and there is little, if any, reflection. Learning is motivated by external factors such as demands from employers or assessment requirements.

How?

Deep approach: This involves critically analysing new ideas and linking them with existing and wider knowledge. This approach means the learner will understand and be able to apply the learning in new and different contexts. Deep learning assists with problem solving and making wider connections.

It is vital to take a 'deep approach' to theory informed practice. When considering the theory that informs their practice, practitioners need to be able to do much more than simply name a theory. They need to take this deeper and think about:

- How they applied and used each theory
- What worked and what they might do differently in their application of a theory in future
- What other theories may have been relevant to a situation or individual and why they chose not to use these

Taking a deeper approach to theory informed practice also involves:

- reflecting on practice to develop ideas and theories
- checking the practice validity of theory through taking a critical stance
- considering the relationship of theory to other knowledge

How?

Beware!

Surface approaches to theory informed practice are potentially dangerous. For example, as Lombardozzi (2009) states:

"once you reduce theories to bullet points, it's very easy for us to forget what the underlying concepts really mean. Individuals who never learned the underlying theory may also misinterpret a bullet point - albeit with good intentions."

Some of the exercises / ideas presented in this Pocket Guide can be used on a surface level which will not lead to improved practice. Do make sure you use any such exercises as a beginning point for deeper learning.

Techniques and Exercises for Developing Theory Informed Practice

As a practice educator and a trainer, I work with social workers and students who want to find practical ways of developing their skills in theory informed practice. Working with students, practice educators and social workers, we have discovered and developed a number of techniques and models which can help practitioners to further develop their skills in this area. These are explained in the following pages of the Pocket Guide. A variety of different approaches are available and different practitioners will find different models appealing. It's worth trying the variety out and seeing which you find the most useful.

How?

"Fiona's model"

I learn a great deal from the students I work with and I enjoy the challenges of discussing and debating their experiences of theory informed practice. A student I worked with recently used a method of preparing for these discussions that I thought was really useful and I asked for her permission to share this with others.

Fiona prepared a couple of pages on a different theory or model for each supervision session. Each piece of paper was split in half - on the left hand side she detailed some of the basic concepts and ideas in the theory (recognising that a theory is essentially a set of ideas). On the right hand side of the paper, she prepared some notes on how these ideas could be used in her practice. As the placement progressed, Fiona was able to develop her notes on the right hand side to consider in what ways the ideas didn't work and to note her own ideas about how her practice could develop. In this way, she moved from linking theory, to applying theory and checking its validity to theorising on her own practice. A simple but effective idea that really worked.

Theory Circles

I find theory circles (which in many ways reflect the social work process) useful in considering how we can utilise theory in practice:

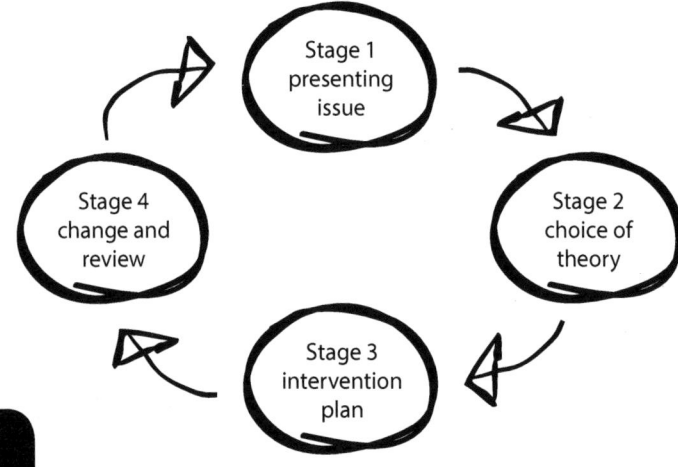

How?

The idea of theory circles is that the circle illustrates the fact that when faced with a situation (the presenting issue in Stage 1), practitioners consider the issue using an understanding of theory (Stage 2) to develop their action plan (Stage 3).

Stage 2, however, is very often subconscious - such that practitioners work in a way which reflects "What is the issue? and What can I do about it". This can mean that the practitioner does not recognise that Stage 3 (their action plan) is in fact informed by Stage 2 (their theory base).

Whenever a practitioner considers a presenting issue and decides on a plan, they have used a theory. The fact that different practitioners may decide on different forms of intervention illustrates this clearly. To provide an example of this, consider a situation where a social worker is working with someone who has behaviour which is described as challenging or difficult to manage. The worker could take a variety of approaches, each of which would have been informed by a different theory (whether the worker recognises this or not!) The following theory circles help to illustrate the point:

Example 1:

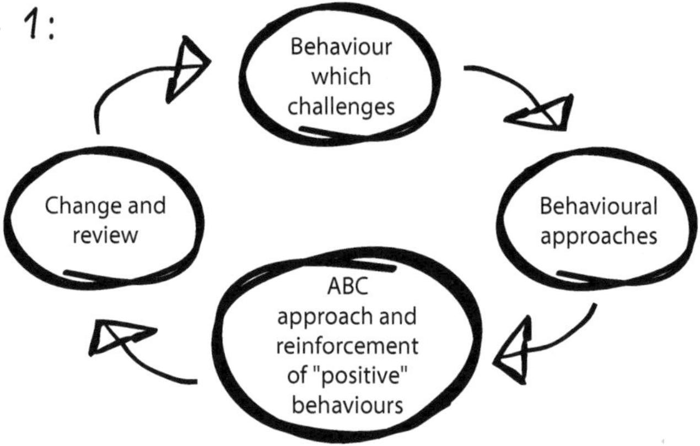

- Behaviour which challenges
- Behavioural approaches
- ABC approach and reinforcement of "positive" behaviours
- Change and review

In this example, the worker uses an approach looking at the antecedents to the behaviour and the consequences of the behaviour. They then look for ways to reinforce behaviour which is seen as more socially acceptable. Whether they recognise it or not, this worker is drawing on behaviourism as their theory base.

How?

Example 2:

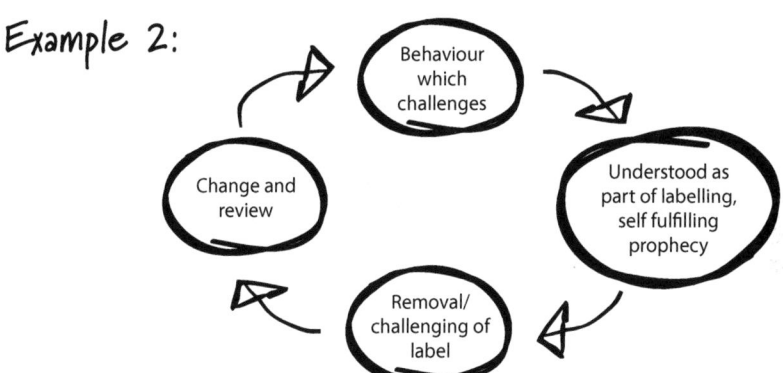

In this example, the worker believes that the service user has been 'labelled'. Perhaps others around the person are responding to them in a way which causes more "difficult" behaviours. The person is "living out" their label. The worker tries to remove the label and challenge those who respond to the person in this way. The practitioner is drawing on an understanding of labelling processes and the self fulfilling prophecy.

Example 3:

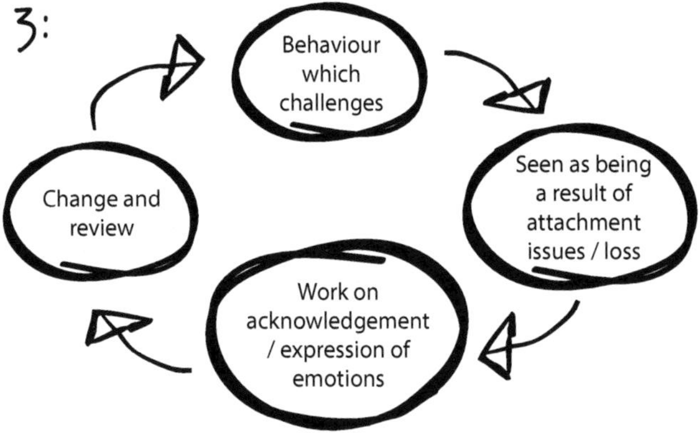

- Behaviour which challenges
- Seen as being a result of attachment issues / loss
- Work on acknowledgement / expression of emotions
- Change and review

In this situation, the worker sees the behaviour as a form of communication by the service user. They may look to supporting the service user to express their emotions and communicate in a more socially acceptable way. They may be drawing on an understanding of loss or attachment difficulties.

How?

Example 4:

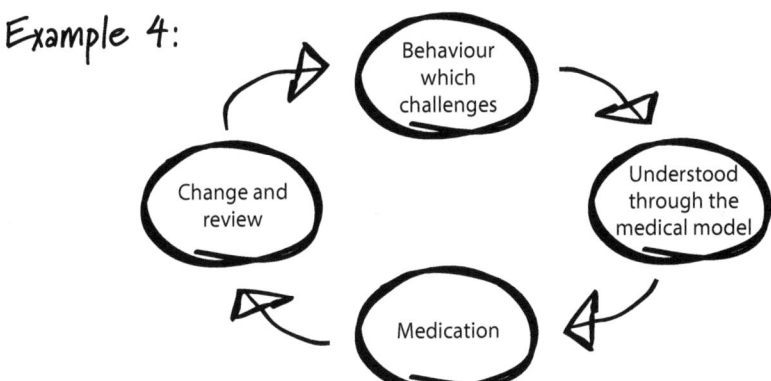

In this situation, the response to the behaviour which is challenging is to medicate the individual. This response is drawn from the worker using a medical model approach, "diagnosing" the individual and seeing the behaviour as a set of symptoms. The person needs to be "cured" and the practitioner supports the use of medication to achieve this.

Example 5:

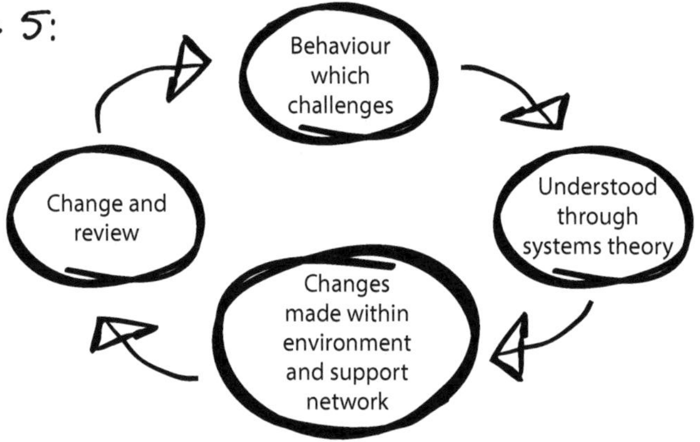

- Behaviour which challenges
- Understood through systems theory
- Changes made within environment and support network
- Change and review

In this situation, the worker views the behaviour in terms of the person's environment and relationships. They feel that if they make some changes within this, the behaviour might change. They are drawing on their understanding of systems theory.

How?

Example 6:

The worker responds to the service user by recognising them as the expert on their own situation, supporting them to develop their own resources and finding new ways of responding to the oppressive situation they are in. In this situation, the practitioner has seen the behaviour as the result of power dynamics and the service user's experiences of oppression.

'Listing' Theories

Most people favour some theoretical approaches over others. However, sometimes we are not always able to articulate our favoured models and theories. 'Listing' can help people to identify their preferred models. The idea is to keep a running list of theories - so that each time you have used or drawn on a theory, you write it down (many people find the back of their diary the best place). Don't worry about being repetitive on the list - add to it every time you feel you have used a theory even if it already appears on the list. Keep the list for a couple of weeks - over which time a pattern should emerge with some theories appearing regularly.

Simply having a list of theories, though, doesn't mean that we are making the links with practice. It simply enables practitioners to identify their favoured models. It is essential that practitioners then utilise critical thinking and reflective practice to delve deeper into their theoretical choices.

How?

The danger with the 'listing theories' approach is that it may become little more than a shopping list. Theory informed practice can be misinterpreted, and taken no further than the 'shopping list'. I've seen a number of supervision sessions where practice educators have asked a student "and what theory are you using there?" The student replies "task centred practice and crisis intervention." The practice educator writes it down and moves on! That's not theory informed practice - it's plucking a couple of chapter titles from a book.

There lies the danger in this approach. The list must be followed by critical reflection. You will only develop your skills further by using the list you have developed simply as a starting point and asking yourself questions such as:

- Why does that theory appear so many times?
- What is it I find useful about that theory?
- Am I making use of both theories *of* social work and theories *for* social work?
- Why does this theory not appear at all?

'Bullet Pointing' Theory

Another exercise which can be useful in developing theory informed practice in a particular case is to consider four areas:

→ Service user identity
→ Presenting issues (the reason for social work involvement)
→ Work to be undertaken (your action / intervention plan)
→ Agency context (this is the one area which will remain the same - as long as your work environment remains the same)

Then you simply make some key bullet points against each of the four areas:

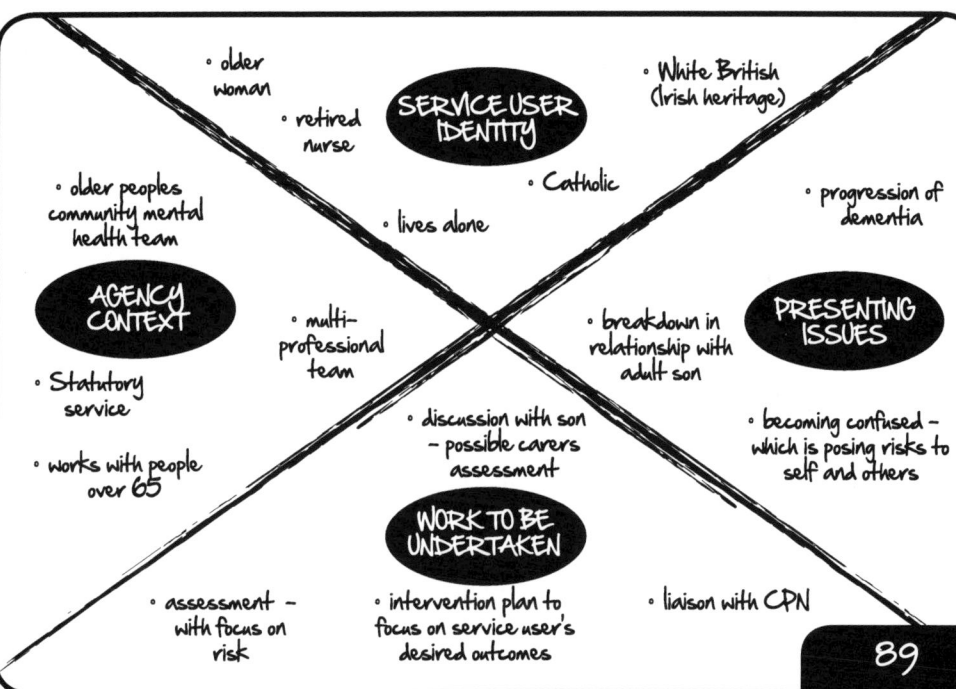

The idea is that you then work through each of the four sections looking at each bullet point, then jot down which theories might have something useful to say about that particular area, which models might be helpful in developing an intervention plan. I tend to use different coloured pens - so the bullet points are in black ink and the theories and models which might be useful, are in red ink.

When working through the bullet points, it is important to think about / identify which theories *might* be related, as opposed to which you have actually drawn on.

This gives you a visual representation of what theories might be useful. Of course, then it is important to take this deeper and think about how the theories might be used, what difficulties there might be, why you haven't drawn on some of those that might be useful etc. The paper simply provides a starting point for a deeper reflection on theory.

I have seen some students and practitioners use this method as a framework to take the analysis of intervention further - using a flipchart sheet they have added different dimensions to each bullet point in different colours.

How?

For example, what legislation and policy might be relevant? What values issues apply? What research might be available? etc. When asked to write a case study or reflective account relating to a specific case, it can also be useful to look at the learning outcomes and marking criteria and add these in too.

Many have found this exercise useful as a skeleton plan for assignment writing when asked to reflect on a particular case or piece of work. Be prepared though - you needs lots of different coloured pens!

Collingwood's Three-Stage Theory Framework

Pat Collingwood's work in developing a framework to support social work students to develop theory informed practice is very well known in practice education. Many practice educators and students I work with find this an excellent visual model and it is certainly worth researching the framework more fully. There is a great deal available on the internet about the model, and examples of its use.

Collingwood (2005) bases the model on her view that there are two theoretical routes in social work practice:

1. A theoretical knowledge base that equips the social worker with an understanding of the service user's situation (effectively theories *for* social work).
2. A practice literature that enables the social worker to intervene in the service user's situation (effectively theories *of* social work).

How?

The framework involves three stages for the student or practitioner to work through, as follows:

Stage 1:
- the service user's profile
- the organisational setting
- the referral

working through these areas you identify key issues and begin to reflect on these

Stage 2:
- theory to inform
- theory to intervene

looking at Stage 1, you begin to consider what theories might be useful in this situation and how you could use them

Stage 3: Knowledge, skills and values

you explore what knowledge, skills and values will be useful in this situation

Howe's Question Framework

Howe (for example, 2002) proposes a framework where a social worker asks five questions about a case in order to make the links between theory and practice. This framework builds on from understanding theory in a scientific way, as covered on pages 16 and 17.

| What is the matter? | This assists the social worker in identifying needs and defining problems. |

| What is going on? | Howe sees this as perhaps the most important question of all. It involves the worker making sense of what is happening. |

How?

| What is to be done? | Goals need to be set, plans made and intentions declared. |

| How is it to be done? | The methods and techniques are chosen. |

| Has it been done? | The outcomes are reviewed and evaluated. |

95

Contextualising Theory

Social workers, perhaps more than anyone, recognise the need to view things in context. For example, we always consider service user's needs in terms of their relationships and their environment. It should be obvious therefore that theory needs to be seen in the context of practice.

Healy (2005) states that it is important that we recognise the context of practice:

"Each social worker constructs understandings that guide them in identifying who and what should be the focus of their practice and how they should proceed........... workers need to select and use theories relevant to the context of their practice."

The importance of seeing the context of practice and how theories relate to this is acknowledged in the various models for theory informed practice. For example, Collingwood's three stage model asks the worker to explore the organisational setting and the bullet point method refers to the agency

How?

context. Therefore to develop effective theory informed practice it is important to have a well-developed understanding of the context of your practice. As Healy (2005) asserts:

"theories provide insights into practice but each of us must take an active role in how we use them and develop them to the contexts of our practice."

In terms of reflective practice, it is recognised that deeper levels of reflection involve considering the way you construct your practice. For example, Korthagen (2005) refers to core levels of reflection which involve a practitioner reflecting on their "mission" (their reason for being, or their raison d'être).

To help you make the links between theory and your practice, make sure you are familiar with the context of your practice.

To clarify the context of your practice, ask yourself questions such as:

- How do I see social work? What is it?
- Why am I a social worker?
- What is my aim as a social worker?

- What is the main focus of my practice? Why?
- Why does my organisation exist?
- What does it aim to do?
- How do I fit into the organisation?
- What does the organisation see as my role and the focus of my practice?
- Are there any tensions between how I see my role and the context of the organisation?

Working through these questions will not only help you to clarify the context of your practice, it will also assist you to develop a deeper understanding of the way that theory might fit into the picture.

How?

Visualising Theory

There are two thinking styles - pictorial and verbal.

Pictorial thinkers: are attracted to visual analogies as they like to think in pictures. They tend to be attracted to diagrams and flowcharts and often like mind maps.

Verbal thinkers: think in words rather than pictures.

As theory is very often presented verbally (often using complex academic language) pictorial thinkers can find theory more challenging than verbal thinkers. Pictorial thinkers tend to be attracted to theories which contain images of some form - such as Maslow's hierarchy of needs (Maslow 1970) and Thompson's PCS model (Thompson 2005).

Pictorial thinkers can find trying to visualise theory in pictures helpful in aiding understanding. If you are struggling to understand a theory try "drawing" it using flowcharts, diagrams, mindmaps or imagery of some kind.

Recognising Common Threads and Themes

Many social work theories have common threads running through them, and often different theories suggest similar responses to situations or make common proposals for action.

To further develop skills in theory informed practice, it can be useful to consider some of the key principles which guide your practice. You are likely to find that some of these guiding principles are actually common threads in a number of social work theories. For example, a guiding principle to my practice is seeing the service user as the expert on their own situation. This is a concept which is common to a number of social work theories, as illustrated in the following:

How?

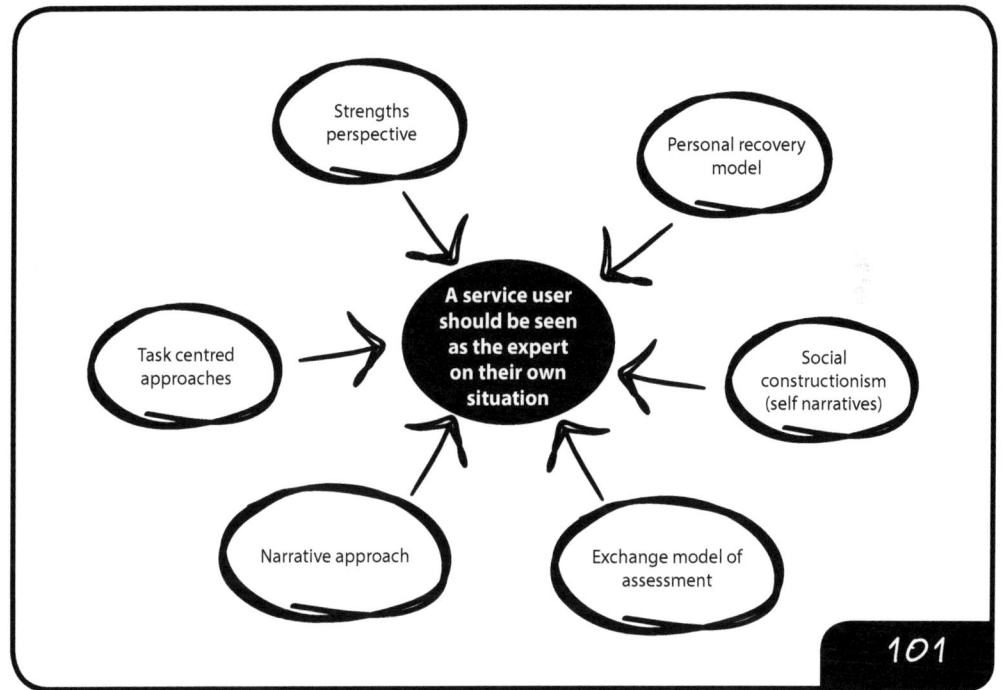

Using an approach like this can help to identify which theories inform your practice. You can take the 'exercise' further by exploring the theories identified in more detail. If one of the guiding principles of your practice is contained in that theory - there may be other aspects you will find useful in your practice.

Models of work can similarly be drawn from a range of theories and models. For example, the use of short term and clearly defined / focussed intervention is a key aspect of a number of social work models, as illustrated by the following:

How?

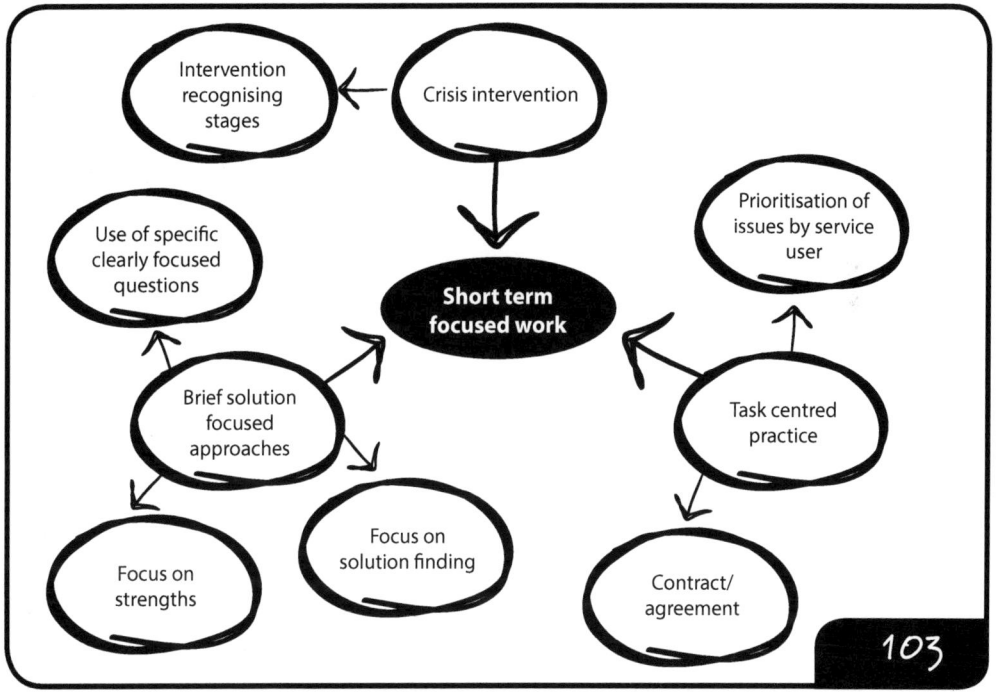

As these illustrations demonstrate, there are many commonalities to social work theories and models and many are closely related to one another or build on each other in some way. This illustrates how and why social workers often utilise an eclectic approach in terms of theory informed practice (see pages 114-117).

Understanding the similarities between different theories and models can help social workers to develop links between theory and their practice. However, in order to do this, you may need to begin by identifying the guiding principles of your practice and the main intervention techniques you use. So try the following steps:

Identify your guiding principles

To identify the basic principles which guide your practice, ask yourself:

- **What do you see as the main principles of your practice?**
- **What guides you as a social worker in the way you work with service users?**
- **What sets you apart from other practitioners - what is unique to your starting point?**

Making the links with theory

To make the links between your practice and theory, try asking:

- **Can you identify any of your guiding principles in theories or models?**
- **Can you identify a model or theory which contains your guiding principle, what else does that theory or model suggest? Could you use this in your practice? It is most likely that wider aspects of the theory will be compatible with your guiding principles so it could be useful to look in more detail at this theory or model.**

Use the same kind of process to identify your main methods of intervention and make the links with theory.

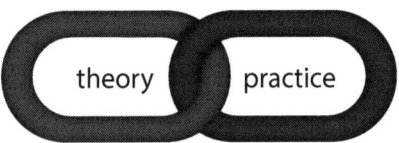

Using Supervision

Supervision is a cornerstone of effective social work practice. The European Charter of Rights for Social Workers (IFSW 2011) refers to the need for social workers to have effective reflective supervision. Whilst the need for supervision to provide a forum where theory is discussed in relation to practice is recognised in terms of social work education and practice learning, often supervision for qualified social workers is little more than a performance audit.

In 2008 an analysis of serious case reviews (Brandon et al 2008) noted the importance of supervision being about more than targets and audit and the fundamental importance of supervision to critical thinking.

Social workers and their supervisors must ensure that theory and its impact on practice is discussed in the supervision arena. Lawson (2011) makes clear that:

How?

"If a practitioner has a supervisor who acknowledges and takes an interest in the [service user] and uses good questions to enquire about what is going on both in the [service user's] world and in the interaction between client and the practitioner, then reflection is mobilised."

Social work must develop more critically reflective supervision which includes theory informed practice. Supervision needs to be seen as *'a learning situation where theory and practice are connected'* (Holmberg 2001).

The need for reflective theory informed supervision is widely recognised in other countries. For example, in Sweden the value of extending the theory informed approach to supervision from students to practitioners is seen as a very positive change. Franséhn (2010) saying *"providing supervision for social workers which recognises the value of theory and uses a model which supports theory informed practice has contributed to the professionalisation of social work in Sweden."*

Tips From Students

Recognising that theory informed practice is a challenge and that very often social work students experience a significant journey in relation to this, I often ask the students I work with to reflect on their learning in relation to theory and practice and ask them if they have any 'top tips' to share with others about how to develop skills in theory informed practice. Some of the tips they have shared with me follow:

- Read as many theory books as you can and identify the one you find most accessible.

- Re-read particular theories and models with particular service users or specific situations in mind - it will help you to make the links more easily.

How?

- Personalise theory - by drawing on your own experiences. It is often easier to make the links between theory and your own life and this can then help you to make the links with service user's situations.

- Recognise that just because you are comfortable with one particular theory, you can't apply it to every situation. Make sure you draw on a range of theories as your skills grow.

- Use supervision - good supervision can help you to test out theories, encouraging you to be reflective and critical.

- Recognise that theories are the tools of social work practice. The more tools you have, the better worker you will be! The more theories you know, the more you can apply them to your practice.

Meeting the Challenges of Theory Informed Writing

Perhaps the major 'fear' that social workers and students have around theory informed practice relates to writing around this area. Assignments for social work courses (at both qualifying and post-qualifying levels) require candidates to demonstrate effective theory informed practice. Many of the exercises and methods which can be used to develop theory informed practice can be used to support such assignment writing. The following techniques apply specifically to situations where you may need to write about theory informed practice.

The three step approach
Try using this approach when referring to a theory in a piece of writing:

Identify and reference the theory
This involves naming the theory and perhaps explaining a couple of the main aspects of the theory and referencing this (generally using the Harvard system).

Interpret the theory in the context of your practice
This involves exploring what the theory and its main concepts mean to you in relation to the work you are discussing.

Application of the theory
This step involves looking at how your understanding of the theory helped you. Remember, you will have used it in one of two ways:

a) it might have helped you to understand what is happening (theory to inform)
b) it might have guided your practice or assisted you in making plans (theory to intervene)

In stage 3, you should provide specific examples to make direct links between the theory and your practice.

Draw on a range of theories

Refer to your use of a number of theories. Here it can be useful to draw on your understanding of what a theory is. For example, it might be worth working through the model on page 16 and 17 to provide a loose framework for your assignment; as follows:

- **Describe** → Give a brief description of the case / work which forms the basis of your discussion
- **Explain** → Why did the situation come about?
- **Predict** → What might be the likely outcome?
- **Intervene and bring about change** → How have you intervened in the situation and what outcomes did you hope to achieve?

At each stage, refer to the theory you have utilised and give an explanation about how you used it.

How?

Highlighter pens approach

When trying to synthesise theory and practice within the assignment, it is worth trying this top tip - which sounds very simple but really works. Use two different coloured highlighter pens. Edit the work by highlighting anything which is describing, in one colour. Use a different colour to highlight anywhere you are discussing theory. What you should find is that the two colours are mixed together throughout. If you find blocks of one colour and blocks of another colour, your work is not making the links and synthesising the theory and practice effectively. Try mixing the colours more fully.

Take a critical approach

When referring to theory within your assignment, be critical. Ask yourself what wasn't helpful with this theory? Which bits didn't fit? Where did it leave me with lots of unanswered questions? etc and incorporate this into your assignment.

Eclecticism

The concept of eclecticism is essentially about making use of a range of different theories. Sibeon (2004) refers to 'intellectual diversity' rather than eclecticism, he believes that:

"rather than theoretical pluralism is an appropriate way of acknowledging the probable inevitability of intellectual uncertainties and complex ambiguities surrounding the contexts of social theory." (Sibeon 2004)

Eclecticism in social work is criticised by some commentators on the basis that:

- too often the term is used too loosely (Trevithick 2005)
- eclecticism does not fully reflect the complexities of contemporary social work practice (Evans, Hardy and Shaw 2010)
- interventions may be based on a mix of theories which have incompatible assumptions (Poulter 2005)

How?

Often, the term eclecticism is described as taking a pic 'n' mix approach to social work. However, taking an eclectic approach is about much more than this. Lehman and Cody (2001) provide a useful framework for what they term a 'generalist eclectic' approach:

1. A person-in-environment perspective that is informed by ecological systems theory
2. An emphasis on the development of a good helping relationship that fosters empowerment
3. The flexible use of a problem-solving process to provide structure and guidance to work with clients
4. A holistic, multi-level assessment that includes a focus on issues of diversity and oppression and on strengths
5. The flexible / eclectic use of a wide range of theories and techniques that are selected on the basis of their relevance to each unique client situation

(Lehman and Cody 2001: 6)

I would add a sixth element to Lehman and Cody's framework - the importance of viewing the service user as the expert on their own situation. This is a common element of many contemporary social work theories and models and fits in well with the current personalisation agenda and concepts of self-directed support.

Despite the criticisms of eclectic approaches in social work, I see an eclectic approach as the only effective way to work in terms of theory informed practice. I would agree with Payne (1998: 130) who says that:

"Eclecticism enables different ideas to be brought to bear, helps to amalgamate social work theories when they make similar proposals for action, deals better with complex circumstances and allows workers to compensate for inadequacies in particular theories."

How?

An accurate and well-developed understanding of an eclectic approach to social work theory is helpful for a number of reasons:

- Practitioners sometimes believe they must use a theory in its purest sense, following the 'recipe' precisely. Often, this is not possible for a range of reasons. The theory may need to be adapted and the 'best' or most appropriate aspects selected for use. A range of other (possibly adapted) theories may need to be used alongside the original theory of choice. This is essentially taking an eclectic approach.
- Most developed professions make use of an eclectic approach in their work. Social work, as an ever increasingly complex profession, is no different.
- No single theory provides a clear explanation of a service user's situation, along with a fail safe plan of action.
- The situations which social workers deal with are complex and each one is unique. As such, service users have a right to expect an approach tailored to their particular situation which draws on the best that a whole range of perspectives have to offer.

See your journey towards theory informed practice as continual

Many social work students tell me that they look forward to the end of their course because they won't need to think about theory informed practice anymore. How wrong they are. I hope that this Pocket Guide has demonstrated why theory informed practice is something that should stay with social workers throughout their career.

Theory can be interesting, challenging, exciting and very helpful for practice. Social workers should view developing their skills in theory informed practice as an exciting journey - linked to the origins of the word (see page 12). Along the journey, a social worker will need to have the tools of the trade with them. A social worker without a knowledge and use of theory is probably going to be as effective as a plumber without a spanner! Theory is the key part of a social worker's tool kit.

How?

> When I qualified last year, a wise old social worker told me, "Time to throw away your theory books sonny, you're in the real world now". How wrong he was. I am constantly amazed at how relevant social work theory is. Not a day goes by where I don't use it to shape my practice.
>
> Being a frontline social worker, we are regularly called upon to enter people's lives and try to make sense of the often chaotic and complex dynamics therein. This is achieved not through any innate personal wisdom, but by drawing on the theories that not only describe what we are seeing, but help us to predict what may happen next. In fact, I think perhaps the most profound thing I have noticed since qualifying is just how much many theories actually pan out in reality. As I have grown in experience, I find myself using knowledge of theory on an almost unconscious level. This knowledge helps me understand the service user's world, guides my decisions regarding a course of action and helps me appreciate the possible effects any of these actions may have.
>
> (Atherton 2009)

- Some theories may compliment each other - but others may clash and may therefore not be appropriate to use together
- There is no right or wrong approach - just boundaries of good practice
- There is no one right way - there are several right ways

Theory and Practice: Sharing the Meal

Two analogies run through this Pocket Guide:

Journeying: Beginning with the fact that the word theory originates from the Greek for "going on a journey". We have considered the ways in which developing skills in theory informed practice is about a journey of discovery.

Food: We have looked at theories as recipes, the need to cook, eating the theory doughnut and choosing the pic 'n' mix sweets.

How?

Theory informed practice brings these two analogies together really well: Journeys can be difficult, you might get lost along the way.... but the journey is worth sticking with. When you get to the point of being comfortable and confident with your use of theory in practice the outcome can be like sharing a gourmet meal

References

American Heritage (2002) *Stedmans Medical Dictionary*. (New York) Houghton Miffin.

Atherton, D. (2009) In Maclean, S. and Harrison, R. (2009) *Theory and Practice: A Straightforward Guide for Social Work Students* (Rugeley) Kirwin Maclean Associates Ltd.

BASW (2011) *Practitioner Symposium. 26 May 2011. Abstract Book* (Birmingham) BASW.

Beckett, C. (2006) *Essential Theory for Social Work Practice*. (London) Sage.

Bibi, A. (2009) In Maclean, S. and Harrison, R. (2009) *Theory and Practice: A Straightforward Guide for Social Work Students* (Rugeley) Kirwin Maclean Associates Ltd.

Biggs, J. (1999) *Teaching for Quality Learning at University*. (Buckingham) Society for Research into Higher Development.

Boddy, J. and Statham, J. (2009) *European Perspectives on Social Work: Models of Education and Professional Roles.* (London) Thomas Coram Research Unit, Institute of Education, University of London.

Brandon, M., Belderson, P. Warren, C., Howe, D., Gardner, R., Dodsworth, J. and Black J. (2008) *Analysing Child Deaths and serious injuries: What can we learn? A Biennial Analysis of Serious Case Reviews.* Research Report. (Nottingham) DCFS.

Clark, C., Dyson, A. and Millward, A. (1998) *Theorising Special Education.* (London) Routledge.

Clifford, D. and Burke, B. (2008) *Anti-oppressive Ethics and Values in Social Work.* (Basingstoke) Palgrave Macmillan.

Collingwood, P. (2005) I*ntegrating Theory and Practice: The three-stage theory framework.* The Journal of Practice Teaching in Health and Social Work. 6 (1) pp.6-23.

Collingwood, P. (2011) *Practice Learning: Integrating Theory and Practice.* Available online at: http://docs.google.com/viewer?a=v&q=coche:4SZhiER97 KAJ:www.ssiacymru.org.uk/media/doc/s/i/Integrating_Theory_to_Practice_ York_Pat_Collingwood.htm. (Accessed 22.7.11).

Collins English Dictionary (2009) *Complete and Unabridged 10th Edition.* (London) William Collins Sons and Co Ltd.

Cottrell, S. (2005) *Critical Thinking Skills: Developing Effective Analysis and Argument.* (Basingstoke) Palgrave.

Croyle, R.T. (2005) *Theory at a Glance: Application to Health Promotion and Health Behaviour.* (2nd edition) (New York) US Department of Health and Human Services.

Department for Children, Schools and Families (2008) *Evidence Based Practice.* Available online at www.everychildmatters.gov.uk/deliveringservices/ multiagencyworking/glossary (Accessed 2.9.08).

Department of Health (2002) *Requirements for Social Work Training*. (London) Department of Health.

Doel, M. and Shardlow, S. (1993) *Social Work Practice*. (Aldershot) Gower.

Einstein, A. (undated) Famous Quotes. Available online at: http://quotationsbook.com/quote/38717. (Accessed 3.8.11)

Evans, T., Hardy, M. and Shaw, I. (2010) *Skills in Contemporary Social Work*. (Cambridge) Polity Press.

Fook, J. (2002) *Social Work: Critical Theory and Practice*. (London) Sage.

Forrester, D. (2010) *The argument for evidence-based practice in social work*. Available online at www.communitycare.co.uk/Articles/2010/06/22/114746/the_argument_for_evidence-based_practice_in_social_work.htm. (Accessed 7.9.11)

Franséhn, M. (2010) *The importance of supervision in social work: the example of Sweden*. (Götenborg) Götenborg University.

Giroux, H. (2003) *Critical theory and educational practice*. In Darder, A., Baltodano, M. and Torres, D. (ed) The Critical Pedagogy Reader. (London) Routledge.

Gray, M., Plath, D. and Webb, S.A. (2009) *Evidence-Based Social Work: A Critical Stance*. (Oxon) Routledge.

Gray, M. and Webb, S.A. (2009) *Social Work Theories and Methods*. (London) Sage.

Green, L.C. (2006) *Pariah Profession, debased discipline? An analysis of social work's law academic status and the possibilities for change*. Social Work Education, 25(3) pp. 245-264.

Healy, K. (2005) *Social Work Theories in Context: Creating Frameworks for Practice*. (Basingstoke) Palgrave Macmillan.

How?

Howe, D. (2002) *Relating Theory to Practice*. In Davies, M. (ed) The Blackwell Companion to Social Work. (Oxford) Blackwell.

Holmberg (2001) In Franséhn, M. (2010) *The importance of supervision in social work: the example of Sweden*. (Götenborg) Götenborg University.

Ife, J. (2005) Foreward to Nash, M., Munford, R. and O'Donoghue, K. *Social Work Theories in Action*. (London) Jessica Kingsley.

IFSW (2011) *Charter of Rights for Social Workers*. (Berlin) IFSW Europe.

Ixer, G. (2000) *Assessing Reflective Practice: New Research Findings.* The Journal of Practice Teaching in Health and Social Work, 2,3. pp.19-27

Jones, W. (1999) *Hippocrates Praeceptiones: Part 1*. Available online at www.persevs.tufts.edu/hopper/text?doc=Perseus:text:1999.01.0251:text=praec.:section=1&highlight=medical%2Ctheory. (Accessed 1.9.11)

Kirkpatrick, I. (2006) *Taking Stock of the New Managerialism*. Social Work & Society, 4 (1) pp.14-24.

Korthagen, F. (2005) *Practice, Theory and Person in Lifelong Professional Learning*. In Beijaard, D., Meijer, P., Marine-Dershimer, G. and Tilema, H, (eds) Teacher Professional Development in Changing Conditions. (Netherlands) Springer.

Lawson, H. (2011) In Cooper, J. *The need for more critically reflective social work*. Community Care 14 April 2011.

Lehman, P. and Cody, N. (2001) *Theoretical Perspectives for Direct Social Work Practice: A Generalist Eclectic Approach*. (New York) Springer Publishing Company.

Lombardozzi, C. (2009) *Applying Theory to Practice*. Available online at http://learningjournal.wordpress.com/2009/07/11/applying_theory_to_practice/. (Accessed 30.8.11)

Lopez, J. J. (2011) *Contemporary Sociological Theories*. Available online at: http://docs.google.com/viewer?a=v&q=cache:JdxbXU3vSGsJ:ssms.socialsciences.uottawa.ca/vfs/horde/offre_cours/0028710205. (Accessed 1.8.11)

How?

Maclean, S. (2006) *A Handbook of Theory for Social Care: Volume 1*. (Rugeley) Kirwin Maclean Associates Ltd.

Maclean, S. (2010) *The Social Work Pocket Guide to.... Reflective Practice*. (Lichfield) Kirwin Maclean Associates Ltd.

Maclean, S. and Caffrey, B. (2009) *Developing a Practice Learning Curriculum*. (Rugeley) Kirwin Maclean Associates Ltd.

Maidment, J. and Egan, R. (eds) (2009) *Practice Skills in Social Work and Welfare: More than just common sense*. (2nd edition) (Australia) Allen and Unwin.

Marton, S. and Saljo, R. (1976) *On Qualitative Differences in Learning: 1. Outcome and Process*. British Journal of Educational Psychology, 46. pp. 4-11.

Maslow, A. (1970) *Motivation and Personality*. (New York) Harper Collins.

McConnachie, M. (2009) In Maclean, S. and Harrison, R. (2009) *Theory and Practice: A Straightforward Guide for Social Work Students*. (Rugeley) Kirwin Maclean Associates Ltd.

Megele, C. (2011) *Defend Munro from anti-intellectualism.* Community Care 15 September 2011.

Munro, E. (2011) *The Munro Review of Child Protection: Final Report.* A child-centred system (London) HMSO.

Parton, N. (1994) *Problematics of Government (post) modernity and social work.* British Journal of Social Work. 24(1) pp. 9-32.

Parton, N. (2011) *Social Work: What kinds of knowledge? some thoughts on the relationship between theory and practice in and for social work.* Available online at www.scie.org/publications/misc/ttswr/seminar1/parton.asp. (Accessed 1.8.11).

Payne, M. (1998) In Trevithick, P. (2005) *Social Work Skills: A Practice Handbook* (2nd edition) (Maidenhead) Open University Press.

Poulter, J. (2005) *Integrating Theory and Practice: A new heuristic paradigon for Social Work Practice.* Australian Social Work 58(2) pp. 199-212.

How?

Sackett, D.L., Strauss, S.E., Richardson, W.S., Rosenberg, W. and Haynes, R.B. (1997) *Evidence-based Medicine: How to Practice and teach EBM.* (2nd edition) (Edinburgh) Churchill-Livingstone.

Schön, D. (1983) *The Reflective Practitioner: How Professionals think in action.* (London) Temple Smith.

Scottish Government (2011) *The Role of the Social Worker in the 21st Century: A Literature Review.* Available online at www.scotland.gov.uk/Publications/2005/12/1994633/46356. (Accessed 5.8.11).

Seedhouse, D. (1998) *Ethics: the heart of health care.* (Chichester) Wiley.

Sheppard, M. (1998) *Practice Validity, Reflexivity and Knowledge for Social Work.* British Journal of Social Work 28(5) pp. 763-781.

Sibeon, R. (2004) *Rethinking Social Theory.* (London) Sage.

Simms, G. (2009) In Maclean, S. and Harrison, R. (2009) *Theory and Practice: A Straightforward Guide for Social Work Students* (Rugeley) Kirwin Maclean Associates Ltd.

Singh, G. and Cowden, S. (2009) *The Social Worker as intellectual*. European Journal of Social Work. 2009 pp.1-15 i First Article.

Skidmore, W. (1979) *Theoretical Thinking in Sociology*. (2nd edition) (Cambridge) Cambridge University Press.

Smith, D. (ed) (2004) *Social Work and Evidence-Based Practice*. Research Highlights in Social Work 45. (London) Jessica Kingsley.

Taylor and Francis Group (2011) *Journal of Evidence-Based Social Work*. Available online at www.tandf.co.uk/journals/WEBS. (Accessed 1.9.11)

Thompson, N. (2005) *Anti-Discriminatory Practice*. Third Edition (Basingstoke) Palgrave.

Thompson, N. (2010) *Theorizing Social Work Practice*. (Basingstoke) Palgrave Macmillan.

Trevithick, P. (2005) *Social Work Skills: A Practice Handbook* (2nd edition) (Maidenhead) Open University Press.

University of York (2000) *Facts, Feelings and Feedback: A Collaborative Model for Direct Observation*. (York) University of York.

Walsh, J. (2010) T*heories for Direct Social Work Practice*. (Belmont CA) Cengage Learning.

Watson, F., Burrows, H. and Player, C. (2002) *Integrating Theory and Practice in Social Work Education* (London) Jessica Kingsley.

Webb, S. A. (2001) *Some considerations on the validity of evidence-based practice in social work*. 31(1) pp.57-79.

Young, R. (1996) *Intercultural Communication. Pragmatics, Genealogy, Deconstruction*. (Avon) Multilingual Matters Ltd.